TINY OBLIVIONS and Mutual Self DESTRUCTIONS

Also by Maxwell I. Gold

Oblivion in Flux: A Collection of Cyber Prose

Mobius Lyrics (with Angela Yuriko Smith)

Bleeding Rainbows and Other Broken Spectrums

Published by Raw Dog Screaming Press
Bowie, MD

First Edition

Cover art copyright 2024 by Lynne Hansen
LynneHansenArt.com

Book design: Jennifer Barnes

Printed in the United States of America
ISBN: 978-1-947879-77-5

Library of Congress Control Number:
2024938791

RawDogScreaming.com

Tiny Oblivions and Mutual Self Destructions

Poetry by Maxwell I. Gold

From the tiniest spark,
an ember glows
until it burns through oblivion.
To the Storytellers
who lit the spark in me,
Edie, Frances, Marty, Walter,
these words are for you.

Contents

Proem for Oblivion

The body bleeds, the mind rots, and in the end there's nothing left but madness whose slime unravels the decadence we proclaim to be reality. Piece by piece, the game is played until we tear each other apart in beautiful syncopation as if the gods strung us together for purposes dictated before primal utterances were ever possible.

It was useless to fight, but only to succumb to the pressures of inevitability, heat, and weight until it started all over again, and again as my body bleeds, my mind rots, and in the end there's nothing left but tiny, tiny oblivions.

Needles and Scratches

i.

They were the scratches beneath the darkest, most impossible corners of the room where only oblivion comforted the endless, painful needle-like sensations I knew to be life. Blood from every cut; bruises, and abrasions colored by skin as if it were some vainglorious portraits.

Needles so thin, like the reminders of incessant, clingy loved ones or nagging household chores, another dim ghost from the corporate muck hoping to cover my salivated brain in bemused promises. They used to hurt, the needles, but over the decades through cruel, air-conditioned lies; numbness became my superpower. Not by choice, but necessity to make dull and powerless the needles, the broken specks of the nightmare that used to haunt me every night.

One after the other, no more.
No more needles,
no more scratches,
but scars they left.

ii.

I preferred scars over scratches, these marks in the night as if petty reminders beneath the humdrum platitudes of dull switchblades which broke the skin so easily; cutting my paper-thin consciousness with rusty insults and a putrid and almost comical sense of darkness that lazily clung to the fog until each droplet was soaked in blood.

My blood.

One after the other, no more.
No more needles,
no more scratches,
but the scars, they left me empty inside this place.

Light and Shadows

Speculation persisted as to what came first, haunting the four corners of existence, atom by atom and embers and stars; without heat or cold, no binary afterthoughts constricted to their lineage. All children of the Void, sons and daughters of Entropy; mothers and fathers by obligations to the bizarre, broken physics which sought to be explained by mad prophets, gods, and scientists who pretended to know the truth of their origins, the light, and shadows, but were easily lost in tenebrific mystery.

These Void Things were nothing and everything at the same time were the old stars whose bones scarred the universe. Their corpses strewn across graveyards which marked the beginning and the end without explanation, the truth condemned to oblivion, lost to the ageless, nameless children in the blackest depths of the what-if and someday soon.

Needles and Smiles

i. Needles

Crooked stitches like grass along the gray-skinned facades and glassy-eyed gods loomed above me. Their awful, drooping lips, swayed in the moonless skies with a crippling, sluggish gait. I'd seen them before, in a place worse than my nightmares where bile and broken memories painted the gray-mattered walls of my tired and fucked-up neurons which lazily clung to the innards of my fractured skull. Needles and patchwork lined the old walls leading towards the open air.

Only rot and ripped nails, curdled in dried blood where cracked bones and sad songs bled through the wrinkled lips beyond awkward faces whose smirk clung to the haze of the sour air. I'd seen this all before, only once. My body covered in stitches like grass along a gray-skinned corpse beneath familiar faces, laughing at the gloom of my death.

ii. Smiles

Beyond those ancient green hills, lumbering under soft winds and broken clouds, they're smiling. Laughing across scribbled and scratchy memories, grey and dim, like light bulbs flickering covered in silvery cobwebs their grins danced with the shadows. No longer confined to a world of what ifs, never wills, or could be's. They existed in a place between never again, where nightmares lay buried under the immensity of dreams and unconscionable terror sealed away behind iron doors of night. Smiling, they were always smiling, imbued onto different faces without bodies, floating in the vacuous imaginative darkness, waiting and wondering. Dreaming and slumbering of something better, something beautiful like tender fingers gently tapping the ivory keys, smiling, a new song carrying them higher and faster until beyond those ancient green hills nothing remained, except soft winds and broken clouds.

There's a Hole in the Sky

There's a hole in the sky with a mouth of darkness prepared to swallow tomorrow, bile and blackness drips from the slit edges of bleeding lips that knew not laughter; only desiccated sadness and hatred. No one cared to ask where the subversion of the heavens began, firmaments scorched with untruth and faulty visions that marched through the streets praising the gaping wide causeways that bent and blasted stars as if they were dust beneath my feet. *Though, what else was to be done when there were holes in the sky?*

Scars never to be healed, cuts to forever bleed and spill the blood of gods and planets through rift and ruin upon the streets below where I'd see the minds of men curdle in rapacious violence, unable to comprehend or come to terms with the merciless doom that poured from the tearful night. One city after the other like brittle paper folded into the crippled agony that was reality with steel and flame as I was the last to know there was a hole in the sky with a mouth of darkness, prepared to swallow tomorrow.

To Follow Orders, To Follow the Flames

Click, tick, and boom, and happy trigger fingers blew waste and fumes from barrel and brains through the woods and everything else went black until the ringing in my ears soon ceased. The world was flipped upside down, the flames were everywhere.

Men in camouflage, plastic explosives painted all around the grand estate warned me of the flamethrowers who marched towards us with intent to burn my life and love to ash. I smelled them, the dark, brittle scent of smoke and char as fire and phlegm consumed our home in dust while the mysterious saviors in camo still attempted to warn us, heralding us to safety through the brush.

Despite not knowing their true nature, I had no choice but to follow. Men following orders, sycophants and psychos who'd do anything to watch the skies be engulfed in fantastic catastrophe, were always men following orders.

There was no other path to take, but to follow the dark, twisted branches, down, down, away from plumes of billowing death and indifferences while the crimson faced harbingers sang their dirges and laughed beneath the clouds of black smog, swallowed in the mythology of yesterday.

Too late, our estates were mired in the lies and music of flamethrowers.

Oh! Holy Orbs How Thine Eyes Were Stars

My eyes were covered in lightning, glassed over with diamond dreams, emblazoned through bloodied visions burrowed deep inside my sad, broken consciousness. And yet, footsteps furiously marching on the other side of dead fields called me not to courage battle, but only to the dread-worry that was the inevitable carnage and carrion doom, blasted o'er the tired winds like the sounds of fat trumpets—low and stubborn. No, there was nothing beyond the trees, the hills, or my tired eyes anymore, but scorched and somber nights barely visible beneath the fog war.

Mushroom-clouded delusions were soon revealed to be nothing but toxic pragmatisms, pulled at the other end of fibrous star-strings—Cyber Gods who laughed at manmade destinies weaved into a nuclear rat's nest of hatred, fire, and blood. Towards the heavens I climbed, my eyes drawn to the darkness as the weight of cosmic indifference pressed harder over every pathetic city down to the crumbling, pathetic brick.

I had been here before, I thought as I wandered the cracked roads where skyscrapers slowly tumbled from the black, ashy clouds as if their bodies were rotting from the inside out, metallic blood and flesh parasites pouring from their marble guts and wire skeletons. Visions of the end, composed through the mad elegance of laughing silver faces ripped my reality asunder like some pathetic rag. And I too, laughed while the world fought helplessly, cackling beneath the guise of the Cyber Gods, as *we* destroyed ourselves.

Black Holes, Beasts, and Doppelgänger Gods

Shifting in deep throbbing nights under a billion restless stars, I wrestled with the stink of rotting banalities, the truth I'd never understood where ashes of my withered existence soared just out of reach, beyond the event horizon.

I usually never won, but dammit, I tried.

The whispers of nebulous philosophies sifting along cracked windows of some ancient mansion, my home of someday, seeping through the vespers where under moldy floorboards, like an ulcer ready to burst, I could barely stand it anymore. I had to catch *him*, race across an ocean of stars, and look into the eyes of someone who saw me, before I was swallowed by this monstrous Cetus of the Void.

Was he a ghost?

A shapeshifter?

Hallucinations?

Dead light?

No.

I didn't pretend to know, but I chased him, through the emptiness and between bookshelves diving through the event horizon, over and over again towards a galactic nowhere, and still, I wasn't any closer.

Don't leave me here. For god sakes, please! There was no reason to think anything might change, only the static and sinister cadences undulating inside the dark as Cetus yawned upward into the night. Soon, I was bathed in a sticky muck of incoherencies, becoming a pile of ash to the whole of existence, but my chase continued for the shade inside a tunnel of depressed spacetime and warped my sensibilities.

Time was irrelevant.

Space was laughable.

All that mattered was oblivion and *him*, shifting in deep throbbing nights under a billion restless stars.

Was he a ghost?

A shapeshifter?

Hallucinations?

Dead light?

No...but the next time I see a mirror, I'll have an accurate answer.

Give Me Your Tired

Where there were Gates of Green and Plenty, stretched along the mythic horizon, ancient songs of fire and lies bellowed into the empty skies. The stale promises carried on ghost ships whose chains rattled in the poison, salty oceans, *'somewhere it's going to be better'* too late they were moored broken and limp vessels. Barnacles and bone covered oaken bottoms of the old ships, dragged across the tides and terror, but too late it was for the passengers who made that deathful journey.

Below tattered canvas a ghastly silhouette of New City painted visions of dread and light across alien eyes. No crowds gathered to greet the death ships, far from Gates Green and Plenty, only the promise of uncertain nightmares and pragmatic monsters who screamed into the night, *'it's going to be better here.'*

A Dementia of Stars

Terrible and ceaseless were the perilous machinations of my poor, broken mind. Wrenched by cosmic humdrums which emanated from nameless forgetful swamps in the darkest places of my brain; I felt the ruin and splendor of nightmares that bubbled in flame and fuckery.

These were the gods that frolicked in spaces before Nyx knew the wild desires of chaos, or Hypnos the awful pleasure that was Oblivion, even the desperate anxiety painted in spectral radiance by Oizys' miserable brush. One stroke at a time, the loss of feeling, and yet, the lights found me in corners beside the bed underneath the stars which began to go out

One by one,
I discovered
the Cyber Gods.

Not in name, but through needle and noxious dreams so heavy, the fog of tomorrow almost never lifted. The Pantheon was remarkable. A dimension beyond my reckoning where brain and body were at the mercy of my twisted imagination.

A Thousand Mirrors

Falling through cracked spaces where crooked avenues raced wildly against neon beams of light; I saw it, the ruins of my life, reflected in a thousand hideous mirrors. There, soon following were the woeful lamentations of voices, familiar and cruel, scratching over the disturbed silences, pulling at the rusty scar tissue of my mind. Faster, without a care, I fell past the reflections of laughing stars, sagging underneath a bloated, fat corpulence that was the night. Heavy and dark, spilling out across existence. The reflections, I couldn't bare them any longer.
Darker, deeper, and faster until tremendous waves of heat and hatred washed over me, radiating from some wretched jagged innards whereupon a foundation of molten glass and iron belched plumes of liquid obscenities. Fracturing the night, rupturing my mind into a thousand infinitesimal shards falling through cracked spaces until I saw it, the ruins of my life, reflected in a thousand hideous mirrors.

Here We Walk Together

I saw a great city unencumbered by gravity's well, climbing into horizons of glimmering steel where towers of strange ivory and gold scratched and pawed at a computerized firmament. Floating inside a matrix of new and beautiful simulations, the reflection of ruin and rot were nothing but bloated hallucinations of dead generations, wrought with indifference and shadow. I had stepped into the light of a new century, where old ghosts drifted lazily in byte and banter, free of parsimonious rhetoric as the grim temples of concentration and slaughter were brought to smoldering piles of ash and justice. No more, no more extrajudicial pragmatism, no more dead rainbows.

"Here we walk together, under the light of black, pink, brown, and yellow stars," came the cheerful voices of a new age.

It was a sight to behold, so worshipful and wondrous as the rubescent auroras sang, underscored by a hopeful tremolo of cosmic strings, pulling and orchestrating a radiant brightness. Their voices throbbed behind a mass of steel, gold, and silicone towers as I strolled down endless boulevards of breathless and bewildered, swaying to the music of new stars.

Black, pink, brown, and yellow; repeating, dreaming and dancing in the lumbering shadows of a city built from the relentless intransigent, terrible hope, whose foundations were soaked in the blood of those who never walked or breathed, "here we walk together" I heard them say. And there, towards the edge of a place that might someday be, were one billion faces, black, brown, pink, gold, and yellow, burning with the smiles of the brightest stars, a great city unhindered by gravity's well, climbing into horizons of glimmering steel where towers of ivory and gold scratched and pawed at a computerized firmament.

Proxima Primordia

The shadows grew long, hungrier as years decayed into atoms withering like dust under the heavy blackness of dimensional and entropic ruin, where wild hominids danced under the frozen guise.of the priestly moon. Though, surging within the deepest throbbing hearts of ancient savages, all they saw was light, intense and hot, like that of a fiery mass crashing down with explosive deadly music into the planetoid below. Curious, eager, and afraid, these creatures stepped closer to it without true knowledge of the thing; though their fear became salvation, howling into the starry night, worshiping and debasing themselves at the stony foot of the smoldering heap of lifeless, diamond sediment.

Within the cryptic silence of the night, the world humbled itself in the presence of the bizarre geomorphic phenom, while one savage, creeping to the rhythm of dissonant environs, twisted metacarpals curling under a yellow moonlight bravely reached towards the rock.
All at once, as if hallucinations from across fourteen billion years suddenly bearing down over a primal consciousness unworthy of such revelations; tossing them back against the crater ledge where inhuman guttural pangs erupted from their chest. Heaving coarse grunts across the aurora bled skies, which stained the night with a horrid lunacy, infecting that poor, primitive race as the deep, throbbing hearts of those ancient savages saw only light, intense and hot.

The Wormhole

I spied the rocks where the most despicable moments in history ballooned underneath a chasm of salt, death, and stars. Across the horizon, I couldn't help but gaze at the horrid aperture whose geometric orifice yawned at me with a deep, primal curiosity. To step closer into the Dark of Inis Mór, that most natural gutted hole with which the wide possibilities of dread and doom were expelled like dragon's-fire into our unsuspecting reality. Closer my eyes were drawn o'er the jagged coastlines, until soon revealed was a dark, silvery face swimming within the star-pus corpulence below.

No, I couldn't help myself, the terror of muscle over matter, brain suppressed by heart-wrenched naïveté to jump and cry under the heavy weight of the dark which boiled in the unlit forges of the neglected dreams. Ahead of me, the foamy waters of the ocean attempted to console my already fragile and broken consciousness despite the bile that pulled me ever closer.

Towards the other side where I saw the end of stars and the beginning of tomorrow, the wanton complacency of truth failed to stay my feet. To ground me in a world without possibility until I spied the rocks where the most despicable moments in history ballooned underneath a chasm of salt, death, and stars, chewed up by the monstrous jaws of Inis Mór.

Promises, Promises

Around the boulevard, where it all began as snow tumbled helplessly onto cities of cement and plastic whose foundations were the oblivion of false gods and flesh toys. Streets grew empty, soon flooded with muck and murder as the thick toxic waters, pouring from the skies, particulates of matter and dead dreams clogged the minds and eyes of pathetic neophytes who walked the boulevards in that nameless, familiar place.

Ash, or snow, useless signified now, made no differences in the darksome realm of tomorrow. I crossed the rivers of asphalt and nightmares, the wind bellowed with flame, forgetfulness, and indifferent hatred which were the only promises in the future.

Ivory Boots, Queens, and Old-Fashioned Nightmares

Thunderous steps tromped through the ruined neighborhoods dripping with pearls of neon liquid, the bloody Old Queens, once glittered with gold and vogue, smiled now through powdered faces and silicone eyes. I watched while they trod along, in drag and dread, beneath the shimmering bloom of flickering club-lights like broken stars, their wiry frames gliding with the shadows in an eerie symphony.

They stalked my dreams and betrayed my eyes, trampling the pools and sweat and excess, coming closer, fuming with gaseous prayers after each step, "come back with us."

Familiar sensations, old ghosts shaking chains from inside a closet I thought I'd banished to the endlessness of my nightmares was suddenly reawakened by each step. The white, silvery boots kissed the black streets with rubber and shame, one after the other, approaching me with terrifying speed.

"I'll never go back..." Back to a world of mirrors, they wanted to keep me, somewhere cold and hidden away, without the truth of self, and varnished in rags and ruin, the closets of my yesterday.

No, I'd never go back.

Still, their gazes pierced my soul with sharp judgment. The looks of not-good-enough, not-dressed-well-enough, or not-skinny-enough asphyxiated my self-esteem with a silky, queer familiarity. The tall, masculine bodies stretched high into the night like bizarre towers, where falling from their lips the plunderful rhetoric continued to blast against my body and mind.

"You're nothing without us.
Nothing but rags and dust."

It grew worse, the pain and footsteps. If I declined again, I knew they'd soon call their hordes of zombified, glittered-up goons to snatch me. Rising from the changing rooms and bath-forges, the fabric-goblins and club-witches, bastard children of the Old Queens, soon came for me.

And yet, the creeping, rhythmic steps of ivory boots never ceased, the horrid trepidation which curdled inside me became worse as time went on and all I heard from across the horizon, "Come back to us..."

I'd rather die than return to a place where mirrors reflect the sounds of thunderous steps and the bloody Old Queens, who once glittered with gold and vogue, smiled now through powdered faces and silicone eyes, at my fabulous, lifeless corpse.

They're Coming

They're coming. A strange mass, unknown, a force only known to me in esoteric mythologies and wild, untwisted fantasies. Faces bizarrely familiar as if I'd seen them before, silver and grotesque that once rose from the salty depths. Monstrous visages which crawled from artificial dens beckoned me to follow them into tubular, metallic innards of the sub-city where I was pulled by crooked teeth who sang, *join us or die.*

Jagged and broken, those calcite daggers pierced my flesh and fragile brain like a pasty canvas easy to rip as it fell to the ground. Nothing stood in the way of that conglomeration of faces.

They're coming, I thought as smiles bled into one another and piles of inhuman skulls smashed against themselves begging to break free of the sub-city. Wishing to pull the rest of us into the body of something truly despicable. Ripped from the stench and grip of the hideous thing, able to flee to the surface, too late I found the streets flooded with false smiles and ugly songs where the stars themselves ran towards the crumbling horizon.

The bloated stomach of the world was unable to contain the burgeoning putrescence prepared to erupt from its unholy, Hadean prison.

A Mouth of Mirrors

Towards the crumbling edge of a hungering abyss, I saw that which was monstrous; swirling oceans of ink, blood, and phlegm congealed with thick foaming waves of rust and bone. There below, a mouth of mirrors, swallowing dismembered closets and hopeless fags like me into an unholy maelstrom of sequestered norms and white oblivion, where light and love were nothing but craggy what-ifs drowning below the crimson, inky waters. The thrashing waters were sharp, cruel reminders of terrible music beating in the distance, trapped between the darkness of choice and another closet.

Lingering in the aromatic stink of the night, a city that never was, haunted by neon queens gliding over a desert of broken bottles, placated by their whiny torch-songs dancing in the tired dead streets. This city, built on the margins of my rattled brain, its foundations planted in scar-tissue and syntax as its signifiers bled through my eyes like broken windows. These were the shades of dead rainbows, wandering aimlessly in this modern Asphodel, pushing others and those like me into that gaping abysm or draining us completely of worth and dignity.

I didn't have much time, or a choice for that matter.

"Since when did we have a choice?" Plagued by my thoughts as a parade of old, dead queens prodded at me through derision and costumed tatters draped so elegantly over gaunt, twinky skeletons.

Behind me, below me, I was still trapped; caught betwixt the mascara and macabre of a city of dead rainbows and the gluttonous, darksome waters below. All at once, slops of syrupy ooze coughed on the edge of the cliff, where liquescent droplets of glass collected at my feet as if it were salivating for my flesh, never entirely sated. Never did I, or anyone presume to understand how the world came to this, the scent of moldy, bleached skin engendered by the night, pressing my senses with heavy, bleak perfume.

No, this wasn't the life I wanted, straddling two worlds, never fitting into either one but, continuously being forced to choose between mutilated self-reflections or a city of closets.

"You made your choices," protesting I stepped back from the cliff, turning up towards the jagged towers of cracked skulls dripping with diamonds and death while tattered shadows and ashy caftans waved like a scabbard, fallen from a sunken ghost ship.

They wanted nothing to do with me, or my words—only the taste of a boy whose reflection was still fresh in the glint of awful mirrors. They were impossibly different, dressed in rhinestones and tears, the shine of their garb sparkled with bizarre reflections of the yawning abysm in front of me. My body reacting in the most profane ways imaginable, excretions of light and fluid unnaturally spilling through my ears. Time was running out, ticking away as the queens of black, brown, pink, and yellow stars tried to flee the dying city, hoping for one more taste, one more bite.

No! Come back! Come back to us, decrepit fingers, polished with blood and silk reached from the glittering dark beseeching me, but there was nothing for me here. I saw their hideous, androgynous forms collecting at the Void of Other, smashed together in a tiny room flung towards the bottom of the universe's distended belly like a mouth of mirrors.

Their desperation grew more ravenous, thirsty, filled with a plutonian urgency as a thunderous cloud of oxidized horror barreled through the cluttered alleyways, toppling buildings, and ripping apart already broken streets tossing silky, caftan-covered bodies into the air.

I saw them, racing towards me with craven eyes, ink pooling into the wrinkles whose existence they would deny, but there was no time. Trapped between dead rainbows and a mouth of mirrors, I had no choice.

Fags like me, never have a choice.

Suddenly, my body was tense, swelling with a numbing paresthesia, like needles in my skin when billowing plumes of iridescent bodies piled in a shimmering mound against me, the old queens pressing me closer to the edge, their profane torch-songs crying in my ears and the lustful mouth of mirrors below. Towards the edge of a hungering abyss, I saw that which was monstrous; swirling oceans of ink, blood, and phlegm congealed with thick foaming waves of rust and bone.

Mutual Self Destruction

Concrete tunnels filled with dirty faces cluttered the crumbling depths with images of a new, terrible future. Revealed in broken glances, metal tears, and salted memories, my blood-soaked traumas were realized as I saw the stairwells clot with flesh and leather when the stampeding masses ran from that nameless evil which sought to swallow us all. Too late, that the artificial pantheons of Faith and Innovation were unable to hold back self-made terrors now personified in radioactive, cyber-beasts forged in a mad-dash to conquer nature; as I felt every footstep shake the sub-city with predacious hunger.

The tunnels would soon be no more, built without a care for the future or the people who inhabited them, they were as feeble as the philosophies which they sought to protect. Brick, bone, and ash filled my lungs despite my efforts to free myself from the darksome grip of my fate.

Hands, teeth, and beleaguered voices clawed at my body. Dragging me back towards the ash and blood. My ears were flooded with bile, my bemused and jockeyed mind thrown against itself like a piece of plastic as the skies collapsed followed by the awful noises of laughter so deep and deadly.

The tunnels were closing...

Ex Oblivione: Nothing Out of the End

i.

Inside the oblivion of sleep, I pressed through the starry gates of never-again where silver daggers scratched at the nape of my tired consciousness. Familiar voices like cackling gods carried me into the amethystine night underneath the guise of stars that were eyes, pulling back the awful realizations bleeding from my skull,

Familiar voices,
and terrible places

I'd been here once before, or two in moments unable to recall within the oblivion of sleep where gods died, and demons cut at my body with rusty knives. I'd woken up a few mornings with blood and abrasions, but recalled nothing except,

Familiar voices,
inside terrible places,

With no way out, while unreasonable gods carried on into the dank galactic recesses as if my pain was some trivial jubilation; the immense shadows encroaching around me, a lethal paresthesia paralyzed my body blasted with,

Familiar voices,

and terrible places.

Places without reason or structure, daggers that reached the heavens with eyes melting from the stars whose crimson slime and purple ooze clogged my lungs and there was no escape. Only to hope that I'd find refuge inside the oblivion of sleep, over and over again a relentless, deadly repetition of what-was or what-never-would-be, trapped by,

Familiar voices,

and terrible places

Trapped in the space between cracks locked in memories like crumbs beneath yellow nails too terrible for sight, but familiar to the mind so fragile, burdened and blasted. Sleep was a luxury unattainable in the world unreachable,

Familiar voices,

And terrible places,

ii.

Soon disappeared through the madness and mania as if the music of molten histories brought by the Cyber Gods was all but some faulty misfire, a stroked glitch in the grey-matter ruins sloshing in my head,

Back and forth,

inside and out

Until there was no more music, no comprehension of oblivion, or even the faint painful reminders of familiar and terrible dreams. The static and somber what-ifs where I longed for the sweet kiss of Oblivion's embrace

grew into not dreams, but nightmares that stained the viscera of my brain,
Inside and out,
all around,
the hideous murals of some far-off Thing who chose me as their unwilling,
hierophantic vessel.
To fill, to amplify, to birth something beyond primal reason, to never
understand but throb within the star-webbed nethers of tomorrow,
Inside and out,
all around,
Until the wide, mass that was Oblivion embraced me once more,

iii.

Until I was broken, nameless, and empty, a vial drained of what was once
blood and song. The days long passed when I saw stars turned to sand,
gods to stone, and now, that bludgeoned executioner who held the
desperate moments of my finality was but, ash and laughter,

Ash and laughter, I've heard it before, all and all
down
this
road
through
this
door
Into a world I didn't belong, but seldom regretted the time spent where
((names)) meant nothing and pantheons crumbled every morning like the
next sunrise and yet there was no answer. Not call, or clarity, but laughter
through doors inside the night in the executioner's palace.

The days long passed, not fast enough though I longed for the sweet glaive of oblivion to sever the insipid neurons from their pathetic strands, my torturous consciousness, it never came; down

this

road

only broken prayers and oxidized snow which sprinkled my lips as if seasoning my body for the hell to come. Come through

this

door

And bring me light. Give me fire, I'd cry, but too late I saw the days pass into shadow and song as I laid against the towers of someday, shattered like glass broken, nameless, and empty.

iv.

Blood and song, sing the music of endless stars,
Blood and song, the anthems of Gods who cared not for tomorrow or cursed yesterday, but laughed in the familiar voices,
Choral chants like ghosts of never-before, or spectral things Shadows which clung to the skies while children remained in their beds, away from terrible men who screamed

Blood and song, sing the music of endless stars,
Blood and song, the anthem that called dark men to places without return beneath the guise of faceless monsters who laughed with bellies full of billions like me. Stars which never shined, nor the chance to sing, but drowned by

Blood and song, to sing the music of godless stars,

Blood and song, the wretched curse of the Cyber Gods
Fourteen billion years towards the beginning of all things as if they were the first ghosts, the dread-voices who curled my ears in the night whispering

Blood and song,
blood and song,
sing the music of godless stars
until stars bleed no more.

The Ruinations of Ad'Naigon

Fourteen billion years towards the beginning of all that was, through darkness and flame; those slimy appendages with hideous scales and silvery carapace slunk beneath the stars. Reaching past infinities, its light unmistakable, Ad'Naigon, the ancient neutron star slowly sank further into its atomic hole as if seaming some unholy cackle where I saw the specks of pallid light descend over the city below.

I had to run. I had to escape, but soon, the light of Ad'Naigon would reach us all though no one dared to believe me. Radiant, spectral droplets as if some amber rain now covered the streets enamored those pathetic flesh-sacs on the tiny floating rock, too late, as the stars themselves fled into their dark retreats afraid of the thing at the edge of space.

Streets soon crumbled; buildings fell like cheap plastic skeletons consumed by the evil that was Ad'Naigon, returned to finish that which it'd begun when Time was less than its equal. I had to flee, despite the futility of my actions, though all at once as if struck by some unknown paresthesia—a black exuberance washed over me whereupon I collapsed in the awesome and spectacular doom that prepared to consume us all. Tears soaked my ashy cheeks as I bathed myself in the burning light of Ad'Naigon.

The Castle Ephialtes

A stronghold built at the peak of my contemptuous thoughts; haunted delusions fused together like steel rods composed that most ancient structure built when man's waning primordia waxed soft under a dim moonlight. Always the keep loomed tall and great, swaying ever so gently in the black muted night, teasing me to approach its haughty gates. Walls climbed treacherously high, bristled tops of cracked stone and chipped marble stacked over one another like forgotten corpses trampled by the feet of armored figures whose yellow eyes pierced the fabric of my soul pulled me closer.

Clink, boom, smack—the chains of infinity rattled as the long wooden tongue extended from its stone mouth as if to swallow me down, deep, through dungeon-dark tubes that flowed throughout its rusty, haunted innards. Smoke and gaseous fumes belched from seemingly living structures as towers, tile, and glass panes shook in darksome belly-aching jubilation wrapped in a cloud of putrid, sour doom. Clink, tick, boom, rattled the chains of night hungry for another body—hungry for me as I passed beyond the threshold; unable to resist the pressure and pangs of my worst nightmare. Bones bending into boulders while my blood boiled away to chalk and charred ash until nothing remained, but the awful colic of my dreams.

The Mesonoxian

Wandering broken streets paved with gold and bone, calcified in darkness, I felt the vast, heaving walls of night, throbbing under a pallid moon. The city remained quiet, evacuated from the bustling crowds and ineffable lights and emptiness devoid of music in the growing blackness which gently suffocated any surviving decibels. I was left in the static embrace of silence, lonely, though strangely comforting. Trash, plastic, and wasted thoughts collected at my feet as I came upon the Doors of Someday, the moon reaching a terrifying zenith casting a shadowy liquescence over the city.

Metallic buildings sagged in heavy remorse, their metal frames groaning under the weight of a thousand long years while I stood at corroded gates. Waiting, wondering when another soul might approach to open them, someday. Suddenly, as if swelling from under the darksome earth itself, a throbbing, pulsing sensation pulled at my brain with a stringing lasciviousness. It was as if the music returned all at once, sounds I'd never experienced, a billion particles breaking free from the sticky, cobwebbed cyber-dark deep inside the heaving wall of night.

My eyes were swollen with tears and blood, while a happy paresthesia stabbed my guts as the Doors of Someday collapsed in a rusty mess of decayed hinges, bolts, and bars where dissonant melodies ripped apart

the fabric of a corpulent night; and my ears bled with bile and jubilance
at the death of emptiness and the sobering of drunken nightmares.
Wandering broken streets paved with gold and bone, calcified in darkness,
I felt the vast, heaving walls of night, throbbing under a pallid moon.

Insidious Trees

My rhizomes dug deep into the bosom of the planet, the bones of trees both broken and infinite. I stood beneath the hulking wood on the outskirts of another settled land, ground colonized, taken from nature, metallic and fake the new graveyards for the Old Watchers who once lazily stalked the viridescent forests and fields. Dark streets cut through felled oaken corpses and metal garters bestrode decayed fungal colonies, fauna gardens, and cracked floral homes where oxidized particulates in the form of ricin and sludge, fermenting these dying lands.

Still, the resiliency juxtaposed against the darksome skies gave me pause as I stared up towards the figure of a skeletal face which hung lazily in the grey clouds. Indifferent laughter bellowed with plumes of smog and gas while I watched the acid rain down over the trunk and tatters. They wouldn't yield in the face of such monstrous, artificial destruction. I couldn't yield, no matter how many of my brethren I'd seen cut down and transformed to brittle, reusable toys for the Plastic Race.

To them, I was nothing but an insidious tree, though I'd remain solid, roots dug deep inside the bosom of the planet. My bones, so infinite and unbroken.

Modulations

So it began with the shedding of self, bit by bit, byte and beast, a loss here, a cut there, something that was expendable. Forgettable. A piece of self, changed to fit the greater whole for the sake of itself. Stardust blown out into the darkest parts of a grotesque universe. Only the smallest changes were allowed, forever and continued like shadows in the dark, lost to me so that one day there might never be another reason to fall or cry in the night, again.

Tabulations

They wanted nothing more than to squeeze the final bits of blood and dust from my fragile body, stuffed inside cursed corporate temples atop some sad hill where the faded grass danced in the cold, dead air. These were the killing fields of corporate monsters whose miscreant excess littered the wastelands of Tomorrow.

What else was I to do? What else was left for me to give? Another per unit, per body calculation forced to produce and balance on lifeless spreadsheets until atoms totaled oblivion, or the lights leveled out into shadows; still piled higher in stockroom and sterile star-vaults, the never-enough calls for progress, to tabulate the costs until time cried to the winds, no more. The bottom line was drawn, and there was nothing left to do.

Termination

Trapped inside a cold, narrow steel corridor, the disembodied ribcage of some dead corporate beast, I knew my time drew nigh.

I waited until they came for me, muffled voices crumpled beneath the static and shadow praying for the end, while others tried to run from the inevitable, hungry blades. Crooked, inhuman, multipronged toothlike swords with blood-soaked tips, cut and carved the expendable meat-sacs into nothing but nameless lint-atoms. Compressed beneath the heartless depths at the bottom of another, multitudinous cyber trash-abyss I was reduced to numbers, bits and pieces of code, degenerated line by line.

There was no room for meat, blood, or the pleasure of muscle here; trapped inside the cold narrow corridors of a disembodied corporate beast whose belly hungered for scraps...for *our scraps.* There was no place for me in the world, so I waited until they came for me, tossing me into the fat, overworked incinerators of tomorrow.

The Needle of Progress

The vile taskmasters and corporate blood lords sat in their crystalline, plastic homes oblivious to the decayed forests, whittled hills, and twisted surroundings. Nothing made much sense in an awful future cut from glass and guts, stabbed in the heart by familiar needles so easily piercing my fragile membranes, layer and brittle layer until crumbling into cheap reusable nightmares; I followed the crippled machinations of history along a conveyor belt towards the big-box-Hell which awaited us all past iron teeth and ivory fingers dug into icy mountains beneath a dying star.

They made me shake, with thoughts so despicable. Towering higher towards the cracked heavens, whips, and wanton cracks like fie whose unimaginable numbers coughed billowy, poisonous clouds into the air. Whatever was left of it, smog and smattered eyes so easily melted into pools of plastic muck, this was the only future now. Stories painted in tasks, true or false, cosmic retardations unbroken, and my body slave to the horror of progress

When Cyber Things Return

Thrashing inside my skull were the awful noises of my life, puerile thoughts trapped in pods of glass and gold, where metal chambers now emptied of gaseous nightmares, laid bare the most sinister iniquities. Bodies drained of water, carcasses floating atop oceans thick with sand and blood like lifeless mineral worlds whirled around a dying star that was my brain; dancing wildly inside an unholy cranial temple, where fissures prepared to rip open the exposed organ to an unforgiving, crumbling existence. Ignorant to the meaning of time, I had long wandered these halls of useless flesh, languishing in the banality of putrid fantasy, hoping for the day when the stars might collapse leaving me weightless, empty, and gluttonously feted, like entropy's sweet little plaything.

There in the distance, scratching the decayed bottom of some nebulous sky, the fingers of a city lost in name, but all too familiar in sight and bone; where the sounds of Cyber Things exploded above silver forges once filled with liquescent dreams, and overflowed onto the wispy, grey boulevards of my imagination. Now, the barren Cyclopean waste stretched wide as if the lips from some dead beast kissing the plane whereupon I found myself asphyxiated by the last memories of a world I'd never see again, sockets empty of vision and thought, placated and humbled before the Cyber Things.

Harder and harder it was to breathe, to think, gripped by the syrupy bile flooding the calcified alleyways, as cerebral structures tumbled into darkness as a sharp paresthesia gutted my body. Pallid flesh and light soon decomposed into dust and dread under the corpulence of night, while lullabies of sweet entropy carried me off towards oblivion; thrashing inside my cracked skull were the last awful noises of my life.

A Promise for Today

When the trumpets of someday blasted across the dead fields of yesterday, the plastic cities whose false promises of tomorrow were forgotten beneath worm and ruin. Dim, anacreontic choirs moaned, their voices simmering beneath broken streets and limp towers where the deranged ideologies of a race long since dead were now entombed in brick and calcified thoughts. I remembered so many awful years ago, when those dissonant tones smashed together in my ears as fire and the stubbornness of flesh met the immovable metallic gods, who cared not for the machinations of our species. It was a beautiful concordance, growing louder, higher until at its crescendo there was only ash and night. There was nothing I could do to stop it. To stop the spastic innovations, bloody promises, and worthless pursuits of self-damnation.

Death might have been a welcomed friend, but that friendship was forfeit long ago, only fodder for the worms while I was cursed to endure a fate worse than any other.

Despite my twisted perceptions, the nature of time escapes me. The circular nature of events had lost its value as most things decay, changing form and function within a cold universe. Fruitless, my efforts will go unheeded for whoever reads this as they wonder about the non-linear logic of a man who was unable to precisely articulate the end of days.

How am I different from so many before me, who heard those great trumpets?

I found myself trapped today, in moments of broken space and fractured realities where the bodies of tomorrow and yesterday were tossed under baneful assurances that the trumpets of someday *will* blow.

Back to Bones

Here we are, back to scratches, complacent with the blood marks on the wall and bruises in the brain which I never understood only knew they were always there, laughing in the darkest fathoms of my twisted nights. The nails grew too long, reaching for the stars only to pull down something worse from the bleak Voids other than shadows which threatened to pull me back to a place worse than my imagination.

Worse than death,
Back to the dark,

They took me, hooked beneath the skin, blood drawn with fiendish grimace plastered across long faces; I was victim and mastermind to the treachery of devilish fantasies which boiled far in the girth and gruesome portals of my wretched brain,

Worse than death,
Back to the dark.

Cthulhu's Grave

The swamp was thick, riddled with broken monuments, inane chirps from leathery-winged creatures atop dead-stumps and empty cement graveyards that once were cities. Useless were the dreams which dared to understand what lay rotting beneath slime and silvery pretension like metallic bones carved from the girth of new stars. Many tried and fell, through thicket and thorny brushes finding their bruised membranes boiled in darkness where the old lights turned away from ancient monsters, coerced by terrible masters too fearful of what they'd stirred awake so many eons ago.

Great and awful, proclaimed those constricted by tentacled prophecies, crippled by the sight of nothing but ghoulish false promises. There, below the syrupy drips, muck, and death of the swamp, no bones, or withered corpse and shriveled pustules from a fable Squid-God or Fungi-Thing lay buried. Waiting for the unsuspecting, naïve sapient to unearth ivory and tusks so massive it might haunt the minds of deranged philosophers. No, the emptiness of a world placated by plastic dreams and cyber things revealed themselves through scorched-earth-fantasies made real, and Old Ones manufactured by conveyer-belt-gods.

Cheap and replaceable, became the stars, too, packaged, processed, and blasted across the ether-spaces of funked-up fiber webs worse than barbarous black lagoons, or the viny tethers of light buckling, atom by atom—there were only dreams and dark what-ifs in the old swamp now; too soon were its waters covered in rusty, steel limbs, unfeeling and cold men who shed themselves of the old masters, disillusioned and hungry, tromped o'er the dead woods.

Terrible and finite, laughed the new gods upon the resting place of old monsters.

Falling into Tomorrow

Faster, or slower, it didn't matter, I felt as broken as the stars, chained down by the fat bulk of gravity. Immobilized by the awesome inevitability which pulled me towards that yawning, depressed middle-infinity. Perhaps falling for what felt as if some inexorable amount of time numbed my sensations, the days bled away into long, starlit elegies whose sparkling music was the only indicator that time had any value. The encircling horizon compressed around my body in star-bones and blood-dreams, painting my tired peripheries with the demented hopes that one day, I might finally reach the bleak, fat bottom; a future too late for me to care.

The lights flickered, and the stars began to go out. Weightless without a sense of gravity, I felt my only sense of time begin to wither into something unknowable and unsettling. Stars twinkled from hot-furies into death-clogs, ashamed of their bloated, flaming bodies, prepared to implode into nothingness they turned away from me. Cursed to fall in darkness, I felt as broken as the stars now, chained down by the fat bulk of gravity, never knowing when I'd reach the bottom, if I'd ever reach tomorrow.

Climate Vomit

Dried up, sandy promises, irradiated nightmares blown through valley-pipes and thrown up into the high clouds were suddenly expelled onto the sullen earth. These crippled words, *someday*, spoken through old lips and whispered as if a lullaby into the ears of a children's future who'd never sing again; watched the toxic-rains, derailed coastlines, pushed higher, unrelenting until breathing seemed almost impossible.

Asphyxiated to the point where the song was only a dream; a faint echo displaced and blasted by the nuclear dreams of a plastic society, the people were stuffed under the bedsheets of the bemused, the naïve, and the blissful blocked by walls of carbon-soaked corpses. Sick, and dried up were the last words like precious water, splashed over the cracked earth as they cried, *someday.*

That Was Epic

Forged in awful plastic cities, remnant pieces of something that once was flesh decayed in rust and ruined philosophies, displaced across some random-access memory points. These placated realities, the broken choices and discarded bodies were the awful remembrances of a society huddled in the shadow of monstrous greed; engorged by the light of progress, too late until the dirges rang o'er the muddied streets under limp metal towers when the skies let loose an awesome and terrible wrath.

Felled by some unreasonable doom, metallic limbs, fiery eyes, and blackened, twisted iron branches slammed into the earth. Bits and brain-like matter grayed in the clouds of yesterday covered the ashy surface of the world. And too late, were the naïve insects who crawled along the thin nimble crust of the world; captivated by the falling stars which wrapped everything in dancing ribbons of heat and a sour, tangerine, aurorean splendor.

Piles of sand turned to glass, and oceans of gold and salt constituted a new, almost alien terrain where the columns of plastic and steel were vaporized in the final moments as the old, yellow star bellowed one last time...*That was epic.*

2055

Filtration systems embodied the permanence of the yellow and orange future which never *truly* removed the smog and soot blanketing the western nightmares; where swirling beneath that smoke, heat, flame, and infection cooked the invincible Manifest Bastards. Meanwhile, across the other side of a glassed and frozen wasteland, a billion displaced eyes wandered under the bright, indifferent gaze of a high star whose position was used only by those ancient white hoods, desperately clinging to their marble ruins, and waterless beds.

No ships to sail; no skies to see; no winds to blow; only the bleakness which washed the waterless shores in plastic bones and metallic bodies, too late to erase the heavy loss. Too heavy for the lungs to breathe, inhalation almost laughable within the yellowed clouds which hung lazily o'er the bronze hills, the bemoaned screeches of hollowed trunks, snapping in ashy death.

Breathing was *truly* laughable now, as the last sprig cried out, deprived not by filtration from the future, but the permanence of inevitability.

I Was Nothing But A Dead Star in His Pocket

I lived at the bottom of the world, trapped in the only familiar place, placated by tired smells, graveyards of pit-stains, and star-dusted corpses. Scattered by the whim of that chiseled, masculine nightmare, I no longer recalled the reason or the origins of my confinement—only the terror which followed as the streets were filled with stupendous cries and bizarre mutilations where he clutched the world in his embrace. We were too quick to turn away from his iron glare, and molten tongue while cities crumbled and the skies twisted into something undistinguishable, atom by atom they faded away into void and visceral oblivion by the awful tinge of his breath.

To anyone else, the godlike appearance that was his countenance might've elicited wild, demented messianic fits of rage and organismic wonder from the masses; ready to please themselves at his feet. It was sickening, which was probably why he kept me. I was never dissuaded by his charm, or hadean appeal. A pet amongst the stars, who too, saw him as nothing but another hungry mass along the endless, icy patches of the universe gloating without cause.

He kept me. Confined in the dimensions and labyrinthian closets he built as if I were his mouse or rat, or worse, constantly running and worrying but without any reason—I never saw the destruction of the planet though, only the terrible glow from his eyes which became my sky at the bottom of the world.

He kept me, and for all the wasted millennia that passed, all the others who perished unable to quench his thirst, even the stars whose light quickly extinguished by this cold, deathly wind—I remained—a dying light as if some failed conquest to the god that would never be, and I hated it—I hated him.

The Redness of Red

It burned away, ineffably, and scratched like nails on a chalkboard, inexplicably hot and cold at the same time as if I were dunked inside a tub of daggers where my screams were inaudible to everyone and no one with colors no longer distinguishable to my eyes but bled all over my body in spectral blotches like question marks unexplainable to the world, but knowable to me—laughing at me—these bastardized marks of trauma, light, and heat inside and out as if staring into a mirror where I saw myself both raw and bloodied, burnt and bruised by the banal pressures that burned like the redness of red—

Seared into my skin, this awful color, another reminder of something I'd never understand, how it came to be. Jackboot monsters marching across the world with terrible faces, one after the other, boots and blood smashed into the earth, flags painted in hate and black swords with red arms, lauded by the Ivory Children. Star blasted and brainwashed, beaten, and spoon-fed by systemic decolorization, there was nothing but bone and char beneath these Crimson Faces. Vile grins dripped with lies, pretending to be champions, when beneath the camo and chants—there were only malignant tumors, monstrous sycophants prepared to spread horrid anthems, *there will be blood, there will be blood!* to coat the world in flames and death until nothing remained of my fragile self, burned away by the redness of red.

Give Me Space

Dark was the night which longed for spaces unreachable, silence immutable, and pits too bleak for words. Endless and cold, I sat in the cushioned palaces at the furthest points of unnamed lands; ancient places spoken only in mythic lullabies where gray shamans sang of hungry gods, and sparkling, hungry Voids. The old stars hung dimly over marble spires whose iron tips grazed the ugly murk of the night, anchored by infinite solitude which might someday find its sweet, bloated relief. Still, I watched the sky with anticipation whose once cerulean glow was now bathed in amethystine shards of planet-bodies and star-bones—all craved space, that which was unreachable, but the most desired amongst all pathetic objects.

Yes, I craved that most sacred and dark sanctuary at the furthest longitude where no songs were heard, nor prayers answered, or even gods were worshiped, and stars remained as fickle as dust of the breath of some monstrous, plastic beast.

Broken was my sight, asphyxiated by darkness, fallen into pits too bleak and loneliness without name like the feverish song which climbed with great volume; chanting in magnificent rapacity, *give me space,* until the trumpets blasted endlessly in the halls of a castle at the end of existence.

When Stars Were Riddled with Termites

Crawling through the infinitesimally small pipes of dread, dropped on my wasted frame I stared at the immensity of choice ahead of me. There, termite infested cellar doors, riddled with hideous carvings like broken fingers dragged along the marbled surface filled my vision. Terrible and beautiful carpentry, so splendid I couldn't help but keep myself enamored with every meticulous chiseled imperfection, sliced face bitten off at the cheek, and oaken bodies toppled on top of themselves like a bizarre cosmic orgy.

Soon, the doors creaked in a horrible symphony, slowly swinging open as the faces themselves almost cried in fear at what they had to keep secret for thousands of years. *Run*, I thought they said with termites spilling from their wooden lips, but all I saw was the fog, shadow, and steel claws which begged, no, reached for me through the spectral haze.

There had to be a way back—some way out of this place; away from the horned beast whose matriculations borne of my worst nightmares dared consume me, again. *Please no!* I cried, staring into those yellow beady eyes, planted deep inside its angular face like pools of dead stars.

Teeth like knives began to gnaw at my skin, the pain too great where all I could focus on were horrendous bulbous eyes which pulled me farther into their darkness beyond the deadwood pylons towards the other side of infinity. Laughter, so metallic and cruel, echoed around my brain as I was carried through rhizomatic tubes by the tiny foot soldiers of oblivion along the winding, rusty pathways to a place where stars rotted from the inside out behind drossy skulls. I knew, there was no way out of this place again, the pipes of rubbish and dread.

When I Swallowed the Sun, I Kissed the Night

i. The Beginning

I marched across the desolate earth, flashes of familiar spectral auroras painted the skies, the painful reminders like bloated songs so dissonant in their harmonies—too late to be resolved—too late to understand the colors the glow from the horizons began to throb, beat, and repeat as if some feverish insanity took hold inside me while along the road I saw the ghosts of what used-to-be cities. Great metal graveyards, jagged institutions simulated only the wild possibilities in a future of fire coaxed through the artificial bot-brains, putrescent twilight-moons, and hallucinatory bathhouses where the stars were like toys and reason felt like a derangement meant to torture,

flash,
bang,
no more sun.

Flash,
bang,
that was the end

when boots marched in mud over manacled destinies,

the alpha-godless-machines constructed from the darkest parts of our own toxicities and engendered what-ifs, spilled from the innards of the great machine, one by one. I stood at the edge of reality, the brown and brittle skies were painted in discolored spectral auroras as backdrop to the heinous, metallic contraption at the center of the city. Metal fingers, masculine and awful, dug deeper into the earth, dragging within its calloused grip the future and flames, consuming every possible bit and byte. The music of somehow, it didn't matter how, really, but scent of iron and blood which painted my nostrils began to fade away and the memories of The Crash were almost mythological as if there was no more rhythm in the world, no shape to reason where words, emotions, even perceptions within the quantum fluctuations as simply as

Flash,
bang,
no more sun

flash,
bang,
and it was too late

when the skies were clogged with fire and death after the stars *really* went out. Screams like a choir of billions echoed across the world, but I remembered, too late, the last survivor of a doomed race where I marched across the desolate remains of a glassed planet, familiar reminders painted the old skies like phantoms whispering in my ear, *you left us to die,* flash,

bang,

No more sun,

flash,

bang,

and it was too late,

to save the world

ii. The Fall

while the stars sank beneath the hills,

they took everything from me, with indifference, without regret pressed into the sullen cracks far below my bruised neurons where nothing remained but ash, fire, and the disheveled, useless body curled into the ruins of yesterday

they took it! Consumed in the worst parts of myself, forged with the beliefs I was *less than*, atomically unreasonable and battered by the brutish philosophies floating in the remnant fogs like some toxic fleck, caught in my throat settling in prepared to cut me down at any moment. The cyber-bastards, they took everything from me, and I'd take everything from them,

flash,

bang,

no turning back,

flash,

bang,

it was too late,

to save the world

From me,

from perception, the tools of useless control for what-used-to-be the bastion of reason like awful, crooked nails along a chalkboard, grated down to the unknowable bottom I looked up with sinister jubilance as I swallowed the sun, knocked from its holy perch, thrown into the mouth of oblivion like

flash,

bang,

heat-death louder than words,

gone, forever

the future

was over like

flash,

bang,

life overrated,

I was dark matter

I was the Crash...

iii. The Crash

Inevitable, unquenched, and cold, I sat on the frozen edges of a broken, dying world, belly full with flame, ash, and metal as clouds billowed high in sparkling cerulean peaks, were soon crushed against my lips.

Salty, covered in the icy cadavers of raindrops and misty faces, I savored this moment; my fingers clutched o'er the tired dusty, earth, prepared to skin the world. No more metal graveyards or plastic cities, or simulated putrescence. *They* didn't deserve the sun, and they'd never have the sky, let alone the clouds.

Self-declared shields as ennobled protection from artificial enemies forged within, too fragile to peer beyond the gray hills, melted cities, and dead forests, but

that time
was gone, now like

Flash,
bang,
glassed over, nuclear kisses,
gone, forever,

the future was

edged over the horizon where the same clouds begged me for relief, even death, their bodies transformed into toxic rain-corpses spread across a broken world they'd never see

flash,
bang,
overrated,

their time

was over, now,

I was the Crash.

No, that was too easy, too good for them; they were mine, forever, compressed by the awful weight of a billion stars beneath my lips as I swallowed the ruined, purpled night.

Their time

was over, now,

I *am* the Crash.

Refrigerated Nightmares

Packed deep inside the high freezers of yesterday were falsehoods, rumors, and twisted thoughts which melted under the hot stars of tomorrow. My wild dreams, perspiring with tears of someday, dripped along the hinges of that frozen gateway where the warmth of something familiar gnawed away at my mind like some nasty little monster. Inside this cold desert, I saw the unending creation and destruction of iced cities, nameless beasts, and skies without a starless crown swallowed by the birth and death from my own sleepless nights; chopped at the head from the scorching horizons like a bloody stump; filled with pus and death. Over and over, I relived these nights of cold, emotionless confinement within the oblivion of my thoughts, my body falling towards the perilous, molten tomorrow as the ice deserts turned to boiling oceans, pathetic gods atomized by the pressures of heat and entropy.

Something familiar, cold and hot at the same time dried my flesh where soon, I felt the sharpness of a someday so dreadful as it clutched my throat heavily, happily, and I accepted its embrace with a cracked smile.

Out of the Mirrors, Fell Bodies of Blood

Crippled, bruised, and blackened were the bones forsaken by my worst nightmares—thrown into glassy mouths, and lost in a stomach of hateful, thick bile. I'd been here before, chained down by memories I thought might never haunt me again, but there at the end of mind, tangled in fibrous, wicked strands—the intrusions of Tomorrow pressed hard on my tired skull.

Get out, they called.
They laughed, *no one wants you.*
Stay with us, they hissed, *no one needs you.*

I slid deeper inside, until there were no more mouths, or mirrors, or walls, but only the high, fleshy portraits which painted my eyes with wild visions of what-might-be through bizarre smiles of the Mirrored Ones. My bloodied fingers and legs clung desperately at the edge of glassy teeth, the scent of salt and death like foul dreams coated my nostrils.

You belong to us, they called.
They laughed, *no one wants you.*
no one needs you.

No, I won't go back, holding tightly against the metal-tongue beast while I watched the cities and cracked landscapes below flood in oceans of dreadful gore. Endlessly, immensely without decency a thunderous cackle erupted above showering shards of glass, gunk, and skulls into the starless nights. My fingers were slippery, too wet to hang on, another fallen body for the mouth of the Mirrored Ones.

Get in, they called.
They laughed, *no one wants you.*

A billion forgotten corpses washed over the ruins of the old cities, cleaned out from inside the stomach-closets; glass-vomit relieved by the Mirrored Ones onto the world and washed away, red ribbons, shredded and drained.

No, I won't go back there, I cried—clutched by crooked tooth-rods like bent steel fingers.

No, let me go! I pressed into the frozen skin, but the Mirrored Ones laughed at my futile efforts, their bleak songs rising higher into the awful darkness where even the stars sought retreat from this world.

Glass and blood spilled from their mouths, my body almost cleaved entirely of flesh—muscle and bone exposed—to the star's last judgements. When all became void and vacant, I fell deep into a swirling pool of wretched nothingness, crippled, bruised, and stripped by a living nightmare; thrown up, again and again as if cursed to relive this Promethean hell until the last, cruel day of my existence.

You belong to us, they called.

The Mouth That Cries Oblivion

Nothing at the end, out of the mouth that screams when its over its never
over along the scarred impossible edges of death where ancient
ghosts reach towards that peak which never gets any closer, never
ceases to torture the tortured who wait and cannot rest under the
starless night waiting anxiously for a death that never comes
At the end out of the mouth who calls for relief, praying to gods and
monster ne'er to be seen, or worshiped by the mad, the brilliant,
and wildly crooked thoughtless neophytes,
At the end and out of the mouth they scream enough is enough is
enough for the bodies that were beaten, broken, and bruised, but
too beautiful scattered along nameless monuments in some far-
off world—never to be seen, or heard,
At the end, out of the mouth inside mirrors or worse, trunks twisted and
turned inside-out from blasted woods and burnt philosophies
raised Bridges of Nowhere until none crossed the threshold, again
At the end, out of the mouth-full-of-stars only hideous regrets as dark as
syrup and bile dripped from the teeth and tightly pulled skin-walls
too high to climb, too wide to scale, but terrible in name,
At the end, out of the mouth, cities crumbled by sacred word, unholy
sword and light misconstrued through doctrine curled like fork
tongue by Crimson Faced devils
At the end, the cycle broken down word by word, tooth by tooth boot by

boot where soon the blood and bone which called the anthems to
swallow the stars soon found its darksome genesis
At the end, out of the mouth of jagged Cyber Lords, who declared *nothing
made sense anything more,* chanting over the body that was
Oblivion
At the end, out of the mouth of false empowered spirits longing for
something that might never come awash in fecal metallic bits
which coalesced into the monstrous idealism
At the end, out of the mouth too broken to speak anymore; too fractured
to smile; too twisted to grin upwards at those haughty lights once
called stars; though never too close or vexed to scream when
it's over its never over at the end, out of the mouth that cries,
oblivion.

The Looming Ones

Behind broken, bloodied frames were the worst of all possible stars, fading into long, tenebrific shadows. Scratching along the tattered edges of my mind, frantic, coated with immutable songs. I hated the shrill and unkind voices, which pawed like some sinister feline at the back of my skull—*come back to us*—back to the city unframed in my thoughts. Higher, taller, hungrier they grew with melodies like death-pangs of war drums, beating soullessly against my tired heart. Taller still they grew over glass mountaintops, wiry dark limbs of dead light hung lazily o'er the fat, gloomy horizon.

Come back to us, they crooned in haunting pleas where the old grass curdled in sweet release to death's embrace; overflowing with dreadful lust; swollen moon-orbs colored by the most hideous golden glow rose above my vantage. Water, brush, rock, and wood enveloped by the music of fearful endlessness where shadow-fingers slammed into the earth, one by one, cleaving the world of sanity. Falling upwards as if laws of reality mattered not, into a wide glowing maw, I watched the twisted gods swallow everything.

Pressures grew, my skull felt as if it were going to be crushed like a grape. *Come back to us,* words blended into a singular noise of bones cracking, heat, cold, and familiar songs bubbling up from behind broken, bloodied frames of my used up corpse.

The Mirrored Ones

On the other side they beckon, across the darkest parts of ourselves through the jagged and deranged flipside-ed universes which exist only in mirrors.

Tap.

Tap.

Tap.

Fake smiles, twisted bodies too tall to be human as if spindly glass pieces of grass climbed high towards the stars, dancing beneath the bleak, spectral radiance on the other side, they beckoned for me,

Tap.

Tap.

Tap.

Bony fingers dragged along the mirror's edge as if to pull me deeper over, no, under the surface to the Stygian place I hide from myself, from the world.

Tap

Tap.

Tap.

It wants out, this thing trapped on the other side of Someplace for untold centuries, perhaps longer. Trapped in a world upside down where stars grew beneath the soil, or the trees took root in the sky, and the sun rises in the West, and the Moon's grin has a dark secret. No, I couldn't do that.

Tap.

Tap.

Tap.

Longer, and more insistent were its stares, empty eyes as if they were pulled inside out sucked of what little life they might have had.

Tap.

Tap.

Tap.

They wanted me, the possibility they never had, the choices that were predestined on the other side of glassy-nothing.

Tap.

Tap

Tap.

Let me out of this place, though, they learned too long ago it was safer to ignore the tapping behind the glass.

A Cry in the Void

Deep inside the belly-bottom dungeons of entropy churning nothingness—I waited in silence, alone. Alone with the most infinite of possibilities nestled beneath the calloused fingertips of death and blistered stars, I cried desperately for someone, anyone to hear me. Beyond the veil where the phantoms of ancient stars linger like twinkling what-ifs o'er sad and somber horizons, or the old plastic cities which crumbled so slowly under the flicker of spectral nights. I waited for what felt like a timeless eternity wedged in atomic silence betwixt Voids and Pits, my light waning with each passing age. Still, my tears, composed in ice, fire, and nuclear wrath bled together, strewn across the universe.

Through the destruction of planets, pitiful worlds who knew nothing of my confinement, they cowered at the possibility of what-could-be, afraid of the beautiful, concrete devastation that was the future. And so when the last pieces of existence crumbled into a compressed bite of frozen nothingness, the last stars fizzled into failed black holes; when everyone had refused to hear my cries—I will remain here, fourteen billion years at the beginning of everything where I watched inside the belly-bottom dungeons of entropy, waiting.

Tiny Oblivions

Not

like

this,

were the pleas from dying gods who drowned in ink, stars, and blood. The familiar throngs I'd hear in my undulating nightmares, a Promethean hell which awaited me;

not

like

this,

trapped beneath horrid impossibilities that were visualized in voids unimaginable and depths where I'd once bled every truth until my consciousness lay wrinkled in dry skin of depraved, skeletal lunacies;

not

like

this.

Dear god, please, not like this when would the labyrinthian Parthenian whores cease their assault on my already fragile neurons. Looped through feeble flesh-hoops, never did I understand when the beginning was the end, and the end was the beginning, drowning under the heavy tidal flows of mirrored dread where I'd lose myself;

not
        like
                this,

The curse of objectivity and signification were never to be enjoyed or understood, but hopeful I'd find a way through the blood and banishment from existence when I came across familiar gateways, seen this place before,

not
        like
                this,

no, the tedium too fragile o'er broken steps which lead me to forbidden temples and brain-cracked palaces where banshees cried beneath shrill, thunderous horizons—clapped with iron prophecies that bent me, bruised me, and pulled me closer—painfully,

not, like, this. I cradled the bodies of a billion tiny oblivions, the corpse-dreams which reflected my brokenness…

not
        like
                this.

We're Here to Eat You, and Devour the Lights

i. Order and Anvils

I forgot how to breathe, the muscles and memories which connected me to a sense of reality asphyxiated by cyanide instruments too deadly to receive the pleasure of a namesake. Hands too large to be human, or anything but monstrous wandered across my frantic peripheries teasing me, no, dragging me towards the edge of someplace worse than Oblivion.

Spasms like anvils crushed my chest with every thrust towards my heart as I found myself trapped in the middle of my bed, a self-contained hell-chamber of silk, linen, and sweat.

Voices so sinister as if the songbirds from a hideous wood beckoned me closer while tiny appendages danced on the floor, whispers, and cackles,

we're going to eat.

We're going to feed,

ii. The Lights

On the lights,

where were the lights, or the sheets for the matter,
edges blurred into edges without a sense of place or sovereign
understanding as the anvils became heavier,
and breathing was a luxury I craved.
The lights, the sanguine desperation to wake up from this nightmare
when tiny fingers scratched at my brain,
my body their food calling from the dark,

we're going to eat.
    We're going to feed,
and swallow everything.

I knew there was no way out.

The Fall of the City of Skulls

Tired and heavy were the bulbous eye-sacs filled with mucus and nonsense in my skull, prepared to burst at the next piece of oblivion which piled higher over the broken dream-streets that were once a city. Confined to the darkest tissued viscera, lined between blood, memory, and wicked thoughts was a place that used to be a city, where towers like bony fingers clawed towards a starless night as if they might tear the very spectral fabric of existence asunder.

I'd forgotten the countless times I returned to this desolate landscape. Every moment though, my eyes felt as if they carried the inscrutable weight of a thousand unknowable deserts. I couldn't bear the sight through each nightmare where the stardust collected at the edges of my strained periphery as if blood from the oldest stars fell from the mouths of dead gods.

I knew something was different this time. Structures wilted, old towers like pale sprigs were withered into pieces of diseased lumber, unable to function properly within the old city. No more did I recognize this place, nor its dark monuments, only the titanic heap of death and mass grayness which crept onward for what felt like a slothful age.

I grew into something different, my body frail with the bone-brittle laughter of mortality struggling with every step as the skies were soon polluted by an assemblage of putrid lights. My bulbous eye-sacs, filled with mucus and nonsense, prepared to burst at the next crumb of oblivion which piled higher over the broken dream-streets that was once the City of Skulls. Dazed by a thick malaise, every brain-beat, every star-curse an unbearable vexation culminated in the finality of my terrible end.

One Last Proem for Oblivion

The body always bleeds, but no longer here, in this place; confined to unreasonable hopes or futile obstacles of flesh and light. Buried beneath a billion tiny, tiny oblivions who proclaimed dominion over the finite ashes which composed my empty futility, it was useless to fight, but only to succumb to the pressures of inevitability, heat, and weight until it started all over again, and again—wait—*no, not this time* something whispered through the most treasonous landscapes in my brain as my body bled, one last time with nothing left but tiny, tiny oblivions.

Previously Published

"They're Coming," *Spectral Realms No. 19*, Hippocampus Press, New York, NY. 2023.

"Mouth of Mirrors," *Seize the Press #3*, Seize the Press Magazine. 2022.

"Ex Oblivione: Nothing Out of the End," *Cosmic Horror Monthly Magazine*, February 2023.

"Refrigerated Nightmares," *Cosmic Horror Monthly Magazine,* March2022.

"When I Swallowed the Sun, I Kissed the Night," *Cosmic Horror Monthly Magazine*, October 2023.

"The Mesonoxian," *Lovecraftiana: Volume 7, Issue 2, Lammas Eve*, Rogue Planet Press. 2022.

"Proxima Primordia," *Lovecraftiana*: *Volume 7, Issue 1, Halloween*, Rogue Planet Press. 2022

"When Cyber Things Return," *Spectral Realms No. 17*, Hippocampus Press, New York, NY. 2022.

"A Promise for Today," *Spectral Realms No. 17*, Hippocampus Press, New York, NY. 2022.

"That Was Epic," *Spectral Realms No. 20*, Hippocampus Press, New York, NY. 2023.

"When Stars Were Riddled with Termites," *HWA Poetry Showcase X*, Horror Writers Association. 2023.

"There's a Hole in the Sky," *Spectral Realms No. 18*, Hippocampus Press, New York, NY. 2023.

About the Author

Maxwell I. Gold is a Jewish-American cosmic horror poet and editor, with an extensive body of work comprising over 300 poems since 2017. His writings have earned a place alongside many literary luminaries in the speculative fiction genre. His work has appeared in numerous literary journals, magazines, and anthologies such as *Spectral Realms, Weird Tales Magazine, Startling Stories, Space and Time Magazine, Other Terrors: An Inclusive Anthology, Chiral Mad 5,* and many more. Maxwell's work has been recognized with multiple nominations including the Eric Hoffer Award, Pushcart Prize, and Bram Stoker Awards. Find him and his work at TheWellsoftheWeird.com.

www.ingramcontent.com/pod-product-compliance
Lightning Source LLC
LaVergne TN
LVHW051016080826
845145LV00009B/2646